Louis Braille

Madeline Donaldson

LERNER PUBLICATIONS COMPANY • MINNEAPOLIS

For Joe, who, like Louis, is persistent and creative

Illustrations by Tad Butler

Text copyright © 2007 by Lerner Publishing Group, Inc.
Illustrations copyright © by Lerner Publishing Group, Inc.

Lerner Publications Company
A division of Lerner Publishing Group, Inc.
241 First Avenue North
Minneapolis, Minnesota 55401 U.S.A.

Website address: www.lernerbooks.com

Library of Congress Cataloging-in-Publication Data

Donaldson, Madeline.
    Louis Braille / by Madeline Donaldson.
        p.   cm. — (History maker biographies)
    Includes bibliographical references and index.
    ISBN-13: 978–0–8225–7608–2 (lib. bdg. : alk. paper)
    1. Braille, Louis, 1809–1852—Juvenile literature. 2. Blind teachers—France—Biography—Juvenile literature. 3. Braille—Juvenile literature. I. Title.
    HV1624.B7D66 2007
    411—dc22   2006028905
    [B]

Manufactured in the United States of America
1 2 3 4 5 6 – JR – 12 11 10 09 08 07

TABLE OF CONTENTS

INTRODUCTION   5

1. A CURIOUS BOY   6

2. AN EXCELLENT STUDENT   13

3. AT THE ROYAL INSTITUTION   19

4. NOT SATISFIED   26

5. A LASTING SYSTEM   33

TIMELINE   44

YOU'VE GOT BRAILLE   45

FURTHER READING   46

WEBSITES   46

SELECT BIBLIOGRAPHY   47

INDEX   48

INTRODUCTION

Imagine feeling the sun on your face but not being able to see the sun. Imagine tasting your mother's fresh bread but not being able to see the loaves. Imagine hearing your family laughing but not being able to see their faces. Imagine smelling the leather in your father's workshop but not being able to watch him work. This was the world of a young blind boy named Louis Braille.

Although he was blind, Louis wanted to learn. But at the time, no books existed for blind children. Nor could blind children learn to write. Eventually, Louis invented an alphabet that blind people could use to read and write. Louis Braille's alphabet brought learning to blind people throughout the world.

This is his story.

1 A CURIOUS BOY

The little blond, curly-haired boy
charmed his whole family. His older
sisters read to him. And they played with
him. His older brother took him for walks.
The boy showed early signs of being quite
smart. His parents decided this little one
would be an educated man.

Louis Braille was born on January 4, 1809, in Coupvray, France. This small village was then about twenty-five miles (forty kilometers) from the capital city of Paris. Louis's father was Simon-René. He was a harness maker. He made leather straps and reins for horses. Louis's mother, Monique, ran the family's small farm. The Brailles didn't have a lot of money. But they were a loving group.

Six hundred people lived in Coupvray when Louis was born. Each week, they shopped at the market outside the town church, Saint Pierre (RIGHT).

Little Louis was always curious. He loved following his mother around the kitchen as she worked. He went with his sisters to pick vegetables in the garden. He liked to see his big brother work with the farm's animals.

But most of all, he liked to watch his father in his leather workshop. Louis sat near the door. He could smell the fresh leather, ready for shaping. Carefully, his father used sharp tools to cut and braid the leather harnesses. Most of Simon-René's tools hung on the wall. Some were lined up on the workbench.

The house where Louis was born became a museum in 1952.

Harness makers made the leather saddles, reins, and straps that farmers needed to guide their plow horses.

One day in 1812, three-year-old Louis managed to get near the workbench when his father wasn't around. Louis had been warned that the sharp tools weren't toys. But he couldn't resist trying to be a leather worker like his father. Soon he was punching away at a small bit of leather. The work was hard. He had trouble making the tool go through the leather. Leaning closer, he punched again. Owwwww! He had poked the sharp tool into his eye.

Louis's mother cooked for her family in this kitchen. It was the warmest room, so the family also slept there.

Simon-René ran into his workshop. Louis was crying in pain. The village didn't have a doctor, so a local healer tried to help. But the eye didn't heal. Soon it became infected. The infection spread to Louis's good eye. Before he was four years old, little Louis Braille was completely blind.

The Braille family pulled together to cope with his blindness. They didn't baby Louis. Simon-René made him a cane. Louis tapped it on the ground in front of him as he walked. This helped him avoid bumping into furniture.

Soon he could feel his way around the house and garden. A certain number of cane taps told him he was near his bedroom. Another number took him to his father's workshop.

NAPOLEON BONAPARTE

While the Brailles were coping with Louis's blindness, France was also coping with trouble. At this time, Napoleon Bonaparte ruled France and much of Europe. In 1812, Napoleon attacked Russia, far to the east. But the fighting was not going well. Soon the French army headed back to France. Russian soldiers followed. In fact, returning soldiers came through Coupvray. Some of them even stayed in the Braille home. By 1815, combined European forces had defeated Napoleon.

Over time, Louis became comfortable in his home setting. The fresh air and his mother's cooking made him healthy. His other senses seemed to get stronger. He'd sit by the workshop door. His sharp hearing told him who was nearby.

But Louis often became bored. He was still curious and smart. He couldn't run and play with the village children. He couldn't help with the household chores.

Meanwhile, Louis's mother was worried. People with a physical difficulty had a harder time being part of normal French country life. They had no way to earn a living. What would happen to Louis as he got older?

2AN EXCELLENT STUDENT

In 1815, when Louis was six, a new priest began working at the local Roman Catholic church. His name was Jacques Palluy. Father Palluy visited the Brailles. He talked with Louis and found him to be a bright boy. Simon-René valued learning. In fact, his wife and all of his other children could read and write.

These skills weren't common among country people of that time. The priest thought Louis could learn too. Simon-René agreed that the priest could teach his son.

Father Palluy read passages out loud to Louis. The priest chose the Bible to help the boy become a strong Roman Catholic. The priest also read from books about nature and science. The passages talked about the way animals live. Other passages described the planets and stars.

Father Jacques Palluy was a busy man. He taught, and he also took care of all baptisms, marriages, and funerals at Saint Pierre.

All the children in Louis's town shared a classroom like this one. They learned by memorizing facts and reciting them.

Louis listened hard to every word. He asked many questions. He had a good memory and could recite the passages back exactly. Soon, Father Palluy knew he'd taught Louis as much as he could with the books he had.

Another newcomer to Coupvray was the village school teacher, Antoine Becheret. Father Palluy asked Becheret if Louis could go to his school. Blind children didn't typically go to school. But the new teacher agreed.

Sighted students helped Louis get to school on time.

Every day, a sighted student picked up Louis at the Braille home. Louis sat in the front of the class, concentrating hard. He couldn't take notes, like the other children. But he could remember exactly what the teacher had said. Louis could also do math problems in his head. When it came to reading, though, Louis couldn't take part.

By 1818, new French laws had changed teaching methods. Becheret had to focus on teaching students reading and writing. Since Louis couldn't do these things, he stopped going to school. But he never lost his desire to learn.

Father Palluy felt more could be done to educate Louis. He talked to the family of the largest local landowner, the Marquis d'Orvilliers. This landowner was also a French nobleman. He and his wife had heard about a special school for the blind in Paris. With Simon-René's permission, they wrote to the school. They got Louis a full scholarship.

Students at the Royal Institution for Blind Youth lived, worked, and attended classes in this building.

This meant Louis could go to the Royal Institution for Blind Youth for free. Louis's parents weren't sure they wanted their son to live so far away. But Louis talked them into letting him go. He wanted more schooling. He wanted to read books. What better place to learn than at a school especially for blind people?

VALENTIN HAÜY

A Frenchman named Valentin Haüy set up the Royal Institution for Blind Youth in 1784. It was one of the world's first schools for blind people. Haüy also came up with a way to help blind students read. He created books that had words in large, embossed type. The words were raised up on the surface of the page. Embossed books took a lot of effort to create. Because the type was so big, the books also had a lot of pages. As a result, the Royal Institution had only a few books in its library.

3 AT THE ROYAL INSTITUTION

Early in 1819, ten-year-old Louis and Simon-René left Coupvray for the four-hour carriage ride to Paris. The school building was not appealing. It had once been a prison and still looked like one. The inside had a damp, unhealthy smell. But Louis was eager to get started.

Simon-René left Louis in the care of the school's director, Dr. Sébastien Guillié. Over time, Louis made new friends. With his cane, he tapped his way around the school.

Life at the school was tough. About sixty male students shared one bathroom. They bathed only once a month. Meals were meager, with very little meat. Water came to the school from the dirty Seine River. Many boys, including Louis, developed a hacking cough. Rules at the school were strict. Harsh punishments came to those who disobeyed the rules.

The school was in Paris, a huge city that was famous for its painters, musicians, and makers of elegant clothing.

THE HACKING COUGH

The sound of deep coughing rang through the hallways of the Royal Institution. The coughing was a sign of a serious disease called tuberculosis. It mainly hurts the lungs. It often spreads through close contact. The boys lived in a big dorm room in the unhealthy building. This helped spread the disease.

But Louis was learning! Sighted teachers read lessons to the students, who learned by remembering them. Gifted with a strong memory, Louis did well in all his classes. Dr. Guillié focused a lot on music lessons. Louis had never learned to play any instruments, but he was a natural. Soon he was playing pieces on a piano, an organ, and a cello.

Another part of the school's activities took place in the workshops. Here, blind students learned to make ladies' slippers, to knit hats and gloves, and to weave.

Students sewed slippers on a wooden form held between the knees. The slippers were made of fur.

These goods were sold to help support the school. Louis took to this work very well. He spent many hours making slippers. Eventually, Louis became the student manager of the slipper workshop.

Meanwhile, Louis's thirst for knowledge kept building. When Louis finally got a chance to feel the library's embossed books, he was disappointed. The reader had to trace every letter of every word. It took a long time to get to the end of a sentence. By that point, the reader had often forgotten the beginning of the sentence. Louis wasn't satisfied.

This large embossed book teaches students how to read and play music.

By 1821, the institution had a new director, Dr. Alexandre François-René Pignier. And he was open to new ideas.

People often came to the school to talk about a better way to teach blind people. They wanted to try out their new ideas on the students. One of those people was a French army captain named Charles Barbier. He showed Dr. Pignier a method called night writing.

Charles Barbier fought in Napoleon's army. He was an artillery captain in charge of guns and cannons.

Night writing was a series of embossed dots and dashes that stood for sounds. Barbier had developed it for soldiers in the field. They could communicate at night without talking or using lights that could alert the enemy.

Dr. Pignier agreed to let Barbier explain night writing to the students. Then he tested its use with the students. Barbier brought slates and pointed writing tools called styli. Twelve-year-old Louis was among the testers.

Barbier described how to punch the dots and dashes into the slates. Then he read aloud to the boys. Listening to his words, the students translated the sounds into night-writing symbols. Louis quickly figured out the benefits of night writing. With it, blind students could take notes, instead of just remembering what their teachers had said. They could write down their thoughts or send messages to one another.

Louis also found problems with night writing. The system didn't have numbers. It had no punctuation. A writer couldn't tell when a sentence started and stopped. Because night writing was based on sounds, it had no spelling or grammar. Words in books for sighted people were based on letters, not sounds. Louis knew that a night writer would never be able to read and write as a sighted person would. There had to be a better way.

4 NOT SATISFIED

Louis Braille was very smart. He had always worked hard at his studies. He didn't give up easily. And he thought the dot system had real possibilities. He began working on a way to improve Barbier's method.

Each summer, Louis went home to Coupvray. He spent his time in the French countryside. He enjoyed his mother's good cooking and the fresh country air. He always felt healthier at home. In the summer of 1821, though, he worked. He brought his slate and stylus with him. He punched raised dots. He thought and thought. He tried and failed and tried again. By the time he returned to school in the fall, Louis thought he had something special to show Dr. Pignier.

Early slates had wooden backs. The stylus punched too many holes in the wood, so Louis asked for slates with metal backs.

In the director's office, Louis talked about the changes he thought should be made to Captain Barbier's system. Dr. Pignier arranged for Louis to meet the captain in 1822. Louis explained his improvements to Barbier. But the captain wasn't interested in a blind teenager's point of view. Louis didn't give up. Between 1822 and 1824, he played around with the dot system. He had several breakthroughs.

Barbier's system used twelve dots and dashes. First, Louis got rid of the dashes. He then came up with only six dots in two vertical lines. This "cell" fit nicely beneath a person's fingertip.

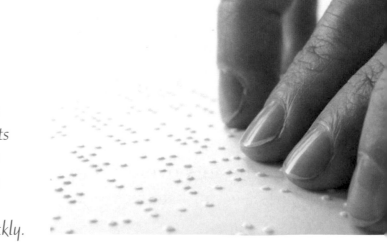

Louis's system used fewer dots than Barbier's system. It was easier to read and write quickly.

The braille slate and stylus have not changed much since Louis's time.

Barbier had based his system on sounds.

Louis based his system on letters. A letter system would allow students to read and write like their sighted friends. In 1824, fifteen-year-old Louis Braille again brought his improved dot system to Dr. Pignier.

Louis told the director to read aloud to him. As the director read, Louis punched his slate with a stylus. He was writing down what Dr. Pignier was reading. Then Louis ran his fingers over each letter and word. He read back the same piece, word perfect. Dr. Pignier was astounded.

Louis demonstrated his system to his fellow blind students. They quickly understood how easy it was to use. Soon the sound of styli punching slates was common throughout the school. The students used the dot system in classes. They also used the new system to handwrite books.

No *W*

Louis's first reading and writing system covered all the necessary French letters. These included the letters that had accent marks, such as *é*, *ç*, and *ü*. One letter the French language didn't use was *w*. Words such as *weekend* and *Washington* came from other languages. So, at first, Louis's system had no *w*. After a British blind student told Louis about the problem, he added a dot symbol for *w* to his system.

Before Louis's system, sighted teachers taught blind students to memorize letter shapes and write them with a pen. This student is tracing letters cut into a metal slate.

By 1826, Louis had become a student teacher. He taught younger students grammar, math, geography, and piano. He also studied organ music seriously. In 1828, Louis graduated from the school. Dr. Pignier asked him to stay on as an assistant teacher. He got his own room and a salary. With this money, Louis bought a piano. He could practice in his room whenever he had free time.

Louis kept refining his dot system. In 1829, at the age of twenty, he published a short book about the dot idea. He gave Charles Barbier credit for first inventing it.

But the world wasn't ready to accept a change from books with embossed letters. In fact, some of the sighted teachers were worried by Louis's system. They didn't like the idea of blind students being able to read and study without them. With Louis's system, a blind student didn't need a sighted teacher to learn. The sighted teachers thought they might become useless and lose their jobs.

5 A Lasting System

Throughout the 1830s, Louis promoted his system. He also improved it. He added dots to stand for numbers. He came up with a way to make music scores with dots. At the same time, students and teachers hand made more books, using what was beginning to be called braille.

Louis played the organ for church services and public concerts at Saint Nicolas-des-Champs (ABOVE).

Louis's career was taking off in other ways. He had become a talented organist. In 1833, he was named the official organist at the church of Saint Nicolas-des-Champs. This was one of the biggest churches in Paris. The church paid him for playing every Sunday. By this time, Louis was also a full-fledged teacher at the institution. He was popular among the blind students. He understood their frustrations and concerns. Louis encouraged them to work hard and praised their efforts.

Dr. Pignier shared Louis's desire to get the dot system approved by the French government. He entered Louis as an exhibitor in the 1834 Paris Exposition of Industry. This show made government officials aware of new ideas. One of these ideas was Louis's new alphabet. At a small stand, people read aloud to Louis. He wrote the words in braille using his stylus and then read them back. Even the king of France came by. He was kind but offered no official support.

Louis-Philippe, king of France, took the throne in 1830.

Meanwhile, Louis's health was getting worse. He still had an ongoing cough, and it had grown serious. Dr. Pignier insisted he see a doctor. The doctor told Louis he had tuberculosis. He was only twenty-six. This serious lung disease had no cure at that time.

Louis didn't let the news stop him. He was still focused on improving his dot system. He wanted it to be used everywhere.

Inventors created strange machines to try to cure tuberculosis. The machines did not work, and some made people more sick.

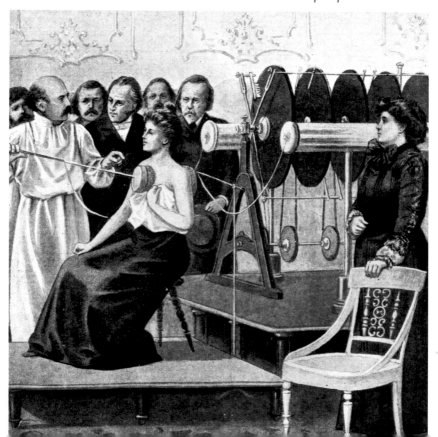

Raphigraphy let blind writers punch out the shapes of letters using a stylus and a special slate.

In addition, Louis began searching for a way for blind people to write that could be read by sighted people. In 1839, Louis came up with a great idea. He called his idea raphigraphy.

Raphigraphy uses raised dots to form actual letters in the alphabet. This way, blind people could trace the letters with their fingers, while sighted people could read them. Louis told a former Royal Institution student, François-Pierre Foucault, about his idea.

The raphigraphe was one of the first typewriters.

Foucault invented a machine, called a raphigraphe, to type the raised letters. The raphigraphe made it fairly easy for blind students to write to the outside world. Louis often wrote his mother this way.

In the early 1840s, Louis taught fewer classes because of his poor health. He spent more time in Coupvray, and his health got better. While he was gone, Pierre-Armand Dufau, a teacher at the institution, replaced Dr. Pignier.

Dufau had long disliked the dot system. He thought a system that enabled blind students to read without help made them less dependent on their sighted teachers.

He stopped the use of the braille system. He took away slates and styli. He burned books that had been carefully handwritten in braille.

Over the years, Louis added special letters to his code so that it could be used in English, Spanish, German, and other languages.

Procédé d'Écriture de L. Braille.
Langage et Mathématiques; Abréviations.

When Louis returned in 1843, the school was very different. As a teacher, he couldn't disobey the director's new rules.

The blind students, however, had other ideas. In secret, they used Louis's system. They taught it to the younger students.

Over time, the director's sighted assistant, Joseph Guadet, realized that Dufau's ban wouldn't last. Guadet learned braille himself. He understood why the blind students liked it. He convinced Dufau that he would get the public's approval if the institution used Louis's system.

GETTING BRAILLE APPROVED

In 1854, the French government made braille the official system for blind people to use in France. Other European countries came on board in the late 1800s. The United States didn't decide on braille until 1917. In 1949, the United Nations said braille was the system to be used worldwide.

The new Royal Institution had more rooms, clean water, and gardens filled with fresh fruits and vegetables.

Meanwhile, in late 1843, the Royal Institution moved to a new and healthier building. An opening ceremony was held in early 1844. During a speech, Dufau praised Louis's system. Blind students showed how easy it was to use.

After the opening, Louis gladly returned to teaching and music. He handwrote more books and musical scores in braille. By the late 1840s, however, his health had again gotten worse. He kept teaching, but he had fewer students.

By 1850, Louis knew he was dying. He could barely speak. He had to stay in bed most of the time. In 1852, just days after his forty-third birthday, Louis died. He was buried in Coupvray. He left most of his belongings to friends and family. But the blind world at large got the best gift. Because of Louis Braille, blind people could learn to read and write.

Many people visit Louis's grave in Coupvray each year.

A Compromise

In 1952, one hundred years after Louis died, the French government wanted to rebury him with other French superstars. These most honored French citizens lie in the Pantheon in Paris. But the people of Coupvray felt that Louis's body should stay in their village. A compromise was arranged. Louis's hands are in a small box on his tomb in Coupvray. The rest of Louis's remains are in the Pantheon *(below)*.

TIMELINE

LOUIS BRAILLE WAS BORN
ON JANUARY 4, 1809.

In the year ...

1812   Louis became blind.
       Napoleon's army attacked Russia.   Age 3

1815   Father Palluy began teaching Louis.
       Napoleon was defeated.

1819   Louis arrived at the Royal Institution for   Age 10
       Blind Youth in Paris.

1821   he tested Charles Barbier's dot-based "night
       writing" system.

1824   Louis showed his improved dot system to   Age 15
       Dr. Pignier.

1826   Louis became a student teacher.

1829   he published a book about his dot system.   Age 20

1833   he became the official organist at Saint
       Nicolas-des-Champs.

1834   he showed his system at the Paris
       Exposition of Industry.

1835   he was found to have tuberculosis.

1839   he invented raphigraphy.   Age 26

1843   the Royal Institution moved to a new   Age 30
       location.

1844   at the opening of the new Royal Institution,
       Louis's system was honored.

1852   he died on January 6 in Paris. He was   Age 43
       buried in Coupvray.

1854   the French government made braille the
       official system for blind people in France.

1952   the French government moved his body,
       except for his hands, to Paris's Pantheon.

You've Got Braille

Braille can be used to read and write almost every language. Libraries throughout the world have books in braille in their collections. Braille presses create more and more titles every year. Easy-to-carry slates and styli help students take notes in class. Electronic braille notetakers also exist.

Modern technology has made possible other improvements for blind people. Using a special scanner, a blind person can scan a document. Software translates the page into braille. A special printer prints it in braille. That way, a blind person can use regular printed text.

A special keyboard allows blind people to read and answer e-mails on screen. Each line of screen type comes up as braille on a special attachment to the user's keyboard. As soon as the reader's fingers have passed over the line, the reader presses a bar. A new line of type appears. Between Louis's system and new technologies, blind bloggers, iPod users, students, and friends have ways to find what they need.

FURTHER READING

Adler, David A. *A Picture Book of Louis Braille.* **New York: Holiday House, 1998.** This read-aloud picture book biography traces Louis's life and gives important information about braille.

Freedman, Russell. *Out of Darkness: The Story of Louis Braille.* **New York: Clarion Books, 1997.** Using a simple style, Freedman brings out Louis's persistence in developing an alphabet for blind people in this longer biography.

O'Connor, Barbara. *The World at His Fingertips: A Story about Louis Braille.* **Minneapolis: Millbrook Press, 1997.** Black-and-white illustrations help to tell the story of Louis's quiet, dedicated life.

Sutcliffe, Jane. *Helen Keller.* **Minneapolis: Millbrook Press, 2002.** Lowery's biography shows how learning braille changed Keller's life.

Woodhouse, Jayne. *Lives and Times: Louis Braille.* **Des Plaines, IL: Heinemann, 2002.** This short biography touches the main points of Louis's life.

WEBSITES

Braille Bug Site
http://afb.org/BrailleBug This site at the American Foundation for the Blind is for sighted people. It explains braille and how it is used.

Children's Braille Book Club
http://www.nbp.org/ic/nbp/cbbc/index.html Books from this website, part of the National Braille Press, are available

both in print and braille. This offers a way for sighted and blind friends to read together.

You've Got Braille
http://www.pbskids.org/arthur/print/braille/index.html
This PBS website introduces sighted children to braille. It shows them how blind children use the system to read and write.

SELECTED BIBLIOGRAPHY

Bryant, Jennifer Fisher. *Louis Braille: Teacher of the Blind.* New York: Chelsea House, 1994.

Henri, Pierre. *La vie et l'oeuvre de Louis Braille.* Paris: Presses Universitaires de France, 1952.

Keeler, Stephen. *Louis Braille.* New York: Bookwright, 1986.

Mellor, C. Michael. *Louis Braille: A Touch of Genius.* Boston: National Braille Press, 2006.

Neimark, Anne E. *Touch of Light: The Story of Louis Braille.* New York: Harcourt, Brace, 1970.

Roblin, Jean. *Les doigts qui lisent: La vie de Louis Braille.* Monte Carlo: Regain, 1951.

INDEX

Barbier, Charles, 23, 24-25, 28, 32

Becheret, Antoine, 15, 16

Bonaparte, Napoleon, 11

Braille, Louis, blinding, 9–10; childhood, 5–18; death, 42; education, 13, 14–17, 21; graduation, 31; health, 36, 38; home, 9; and music, 21, 31, 41; as teacher, 31, 34, 39, 41; tomb, 42–43

Braille, Monique, 7, 12

Braille, Simon-René, 7, 10, 13, 14, 17, 19

braille system, alphabet, 40; approval of, 39; books, 30, 33, 43; development of, 26–29, 32–33, 35, 39; music, 41; and technology, 45;

Coupvray, France, 7, 11, 15, 27, 36, 42, 43

Dufau, Pierre-Armand, 38–40, 41

Embossed books, 18, 22, 23

Foucault, François-Pierre, 37–38

Guadet, Joseph, 40

Guillié, Sébastien, 20, 21

Harness making, 7, 8–9, Haüy, Valentine, 18

King Louis-Philippe, 35

Night writing, 23, 24–25

Orvilliers, Marquis d', 17

Palluy, Jacques, 13, 14, 17

Pantheon, 43

Paris, 20, 35

Paris Exposition of Industry, 35

Pignier, Alexandre François-René, 23, 24, 27–29, 38

Raphigraphe, 38

Raphigraphy, 37

Royal Institution for Blind Youth, 17–21, 41

Saint Nicolas-des-Champs, church of, 34

Slate and stylus, 24, 25, 27, 29, 39

Slipper workshop, 21–22

Tuberculosis, 20, 21, 36

Acknowledgments

For photographs and artwork: © Bettmann/CORBIS, p. 4; Courtesy La Maison Natale de Louis Braille, Coupvray, pp. 7, 10, 16, 24; © Paul Seheult; Eye Ubiquitous/CORBIS, pp. 8, 42; The Granger Collection, New York, p. 9; Library of Congress, p. 11 (LC-USZ62-17088); Bibliothèque nationale de France, pp. 14, 34; © Getty Images, p. 15; Archives de l'Institut National des Jeunes Aveugles (INJA), Paris, p. 17; © ND/Roger Viollet/Getty Images, p. 20; Courtesy of the American Foundation for the Blind, pp. 22, 31, 39; © Musée Valentin Haüy, Paris, France/Archives Charmet/The Bridgeman Art Library, p. 23; Collection of the American Printing House for the Blind, p. 27 (both); © age fotostock/SuperStock, p. 28; © Boyer/Roger Viollet/Getty Images, p. 29; © Imagno/Getty Images, p. 35; © Mary Evans Picture Library/The Image Works, p. 36; © Bibliotheque de l'Institut d'Ophtalmologie, Paris, France/Archives Charmet/The Bridgeman Art Library, p. 37; © Michel Setboun/Getty Images for Lerner Publishing Group, Inc., p. 38; © Alinari Archives/The Image Works, p. 41; © Yoshio Tomii/SuperStock, p. 43; © Pallava Bagla/CORBIS, p. 45.

Front Cover: Rue des Archives/The Granger Collection, New York.
Back Cover: © Getty Images.